I0201697

A

A

IS FOR

ADVERB

AN ALPHABET FOR AUTHORS IN AGONY

ALIYA SMYTH

VARLET ✕ VERTUE

No part of this book may be reproduced in any form or by any electronic or mechanical means, including information storage and retrieval systems, without written permission from the author, except in the case of a reviewer, who may quote brief passages embodied in critical articles or in a review.

Trademarked names appear throughout this book. Rather than use a trademark symbol with every occurrence of a trademarked name, names are used in an editorial fashion, with no intention of infringement of the respective owner's trademark.

The information in this book is distributed on an "as is" basis, without warranty. Although every precaution has been taken in the preparation of this work, neither the author nor the publisher shall have any liability to any person or entity with respect to any loss or damage caused or alleged to be caused directly or indirectly by the information contained in this book.

Copyright 2015 by Aliya Smyth.

All rights reserved.

A is for Adverb: An Alphabet for Authors in Agony

ISBN: 978-0-9948908-1-8

First Edition

Publisher: Varlet & Vertue
varletandvertue.ca

Books may be purchased by contacting the publisher and author at info@varletandvertue.ca.

To the Scribophile writing community, whose countless debates on the merits of adverbs sharpened my agony.

And for my children, around whom writing is impossible, yet all dreams seem a reality.

CONTENTS

- * -

WHAT WAS I THINKING?

———

Like swimming with sharks, writing is an acquired skill. You have to overcome a certain amount of fear to first enter those waters, then to paddle on after realizing you have fresh meat tied around your neck.

Though, after you've girded your loins and taken that plunge, you begin developing a certain familiarity with the circling predators. *Don't use adverbs. Show, don't tell. Too much passive voice. Head hopping! Head hopping!* That's when the agony starts to weigh you down.

Everybody's got teeth. So how do you stay buoyant? Is it even possible?

Writing is a tough game, as it should be—good stories hit us in the head and heart at the same time, and learning to write that double-whammy takes practice and care. I'm a perfectionist, if also a bit of a curmudgeon. Don't sit next to me during a movie unless you want to hear it ripped apart. That doesn't mean I'm not enjoying, just that my cynical side often overpowers my accepting side and beats it into submission. So no one tears apart my work more viciously than myself—though some people have given me a pretty good run for my money.

And you know what? Every bit of it has helped me become a better writer. Not perfect. Never that. But bite by bite I'm becoming tougher and more confident.

Hence, this alphabet.

Once we reach adulthood, our alphabets become less whimsical. Gone are the puppies and unicorns (and always that damn xylophone) of youth. In fact, gone are funny alphabets altogether—until we become authors. Then playing with words makes all things possible again.

These 26 letters are my breadcrumbs through the dark forest. I may look back one day and wonder why I didn't leave a better marker (you know, like some glittery spray paint or something that wouldn't get devoured by a murder of crows). Yet this is me, frozen at this moment in time. I'm putting this strange book into the world in the hopes that some small morsel might lead other pen-scratchers out of the gloom … through shark infested waters … and onto the island of misfit authors.

Write on,
Aliya Smyth
September 2015

- A -

ADVERB

—

When my son started to speak, he did many of the normal, sweet things toddlers do. He mispronounced words, used improper sentence structure, and—most horrifying of all—he ad-adverbed. Yeah, you read that right. He doubled adverbs. His favourite was 'alsoly.'

Are you kidding me?

Also-ly?

I had only been writing in earnest for about two years, and his crimes against words made me think I'd birthed a monster.

You may be a new writer; you may have experience galore. But by now you've probably noticed that the most effective way to start a riot at a writer's party is to stand up, clink your glass for attention, and declare, "Adverbs are wonderful!"

What is it about adverbs that causes a room full of booknerds to lose their collective minds? After all, the adverb is only one of many parts of speech. Its job is to modify a verb, to change the meaning of the action in a subtle, or not so-subtle way. A brief rundown of some common adverbs are:

> *also / only / very / just / and pretty much every word ending in -ly when it acts on a verb.*

The common adverb has become a battleground in a war being fought on multiple fronts, which include the no-man's land of *Passive vs. Active Voice* and the great divide of *Show, Don't Tell*. So, who are these combatants and what are their positions?

Our first army, brightly coloured banners blowing, are the *Lyrical*. We won't sacrifice our lovely, individual voices for one which is conformist and unadorned, they cry.

Next, entrenched in deep foxholes, are the *Direct*. Use of adverbs is weak. Demonstrates lack of vocabulary. A strong, accurate verb is available in every circumstance.

Last, cautiously navigating between the others, are the *Nuanced*. Those of us in this alliance are tired of the in-fighting and name calling between those other cry-babies (yeah, I went there). We recognize (and sometimes agonize) over word-choice. Each is selected with care for accuracy and effect. There's a big difference between someone *speaking softly, whispering, murmuring,* or *slurring*. All those actions could be described as *speaking softly*, yet all are unique. Sometimes *speaking softly* is exactly what's called for.

To-adverb-or-not-to-adverb is representative of a host of common debates among those who love words. Debate can be a wonderful thing. Healthy discussion promotes clear thinking about our story-craft choices. It can lead to awareness of our own habits, and experimentation with different approaches, both things I favour.

However, no matter how passionate or intense the debate, I believe there are no 'rules' which can't be broken. The real trick for any writer is applying your ever-growing awareness of 'rules' in a way which lets you pen the best story you can.

No writer is perfect, and no book will be perfect for all readers. But no matter which camp you belong to—no matter what your philosophy on writing—you'll never lack for conversation so long as you're happy to discuss adverbs over your drink of choice.

Make mine a rum.

- B -

BESTSELLING*

—

One of the writer's most coveted words. The word that signifies success, popularity, and authority. While it might not have the same clout as *Pulitzer Prize Winning*, what author doesn't want to be able to put 'Bestselling' next to their book title or, perhaps better, their name?

Except now, it doesn't really mean a damn thing.

Why?

Oh, a little thing called BLUSTER.

Bluster is common in marketing, where anything that has a measure of subjectivity might not fall under the premise of promise ... like:

> *The best car wash in town.*

The best car wash? Really?

(Excuse the eye-roll.)

Because of our love of bluster, anything that can be shown to be at least partially true becomes fair game. Authors certainly need to market their works, but I personally draw the

line at the following scenario (names and titles changed to pro-
tect the incompetent):

> The bestselling author of
> *The Tiny Stitches of Doctor Moreau.*

How is the author 'bestselling'? Well, they've decided
they're bestselling because they ranked No. 1 for at least one
cycle of Amazon's list of Medically Inspired, Post-Apocalyptic
Needlepoint books. And, by the way, that list is updated
hourly.

I mean, how many books do you have to sell within such an
obscure category in order to be the 'most popular book'
therein? I'm guessing it's going to have to be fewer than 100,
maybe even fewer than 50.*

That's blusterier than a tornado to Oz.

Gone are the days when *Bestselling* had a tiny, modicum of
meaning. New York Times® Bestselling—now that still has
some cachet, even though no one outside of the Illuminati is
certain how those bestsellers are calculated. Likely it's more
complicated than the Explicit Formula for the Fibonacci Se-
quence.

I know authors gotta eat. I know they have to pay bills.
I've been on the receiving end of disconnected power and din-
ners of guess-what-casserole. But I still maintain that it's better
to be an honest, Damn Good Author, than bestselling* any
day.

By all means celebrate making No. 1 in *any* category.
That's a victory. Those can be few and far between for writers.

Just don't be like that party guy who brags about being able to have ten drinks and stand naked out in the cold because he doesn't feel pain … only to end up in the hospital with frost-bitten genitalia. Yeah, until you can claim a true title, please do us all a favour—don't be a lonely nut.

If you ever catch me using *bestselling* without an applicable asterisk, write me some nasty mail demanding I verify my claim to use. I'll send you the clipping from the Weekly World News.

Trust me, it's legit.

---

* Update: Having first published the ebook version of *A is for Adverb*, I now know that fewer than 10 sales is enough to reach a niche category 'No. 1 Bestseller' ranking for at least one cycle on Amazon. Hurray, me! Boo, people who don't use asterisks.

- C -

COMMA SPLICE
AND THE EVILS OF PUNCTUATION

———

Ready for some pain?

> *Guess what if you dont use proper punctuation your ability to create clear meaning which is the backbone of effective story telling disappears in a frustrating jumble of words!!*

If you read that paragraph with a fire of rage in your belly, then we're more alike than you might expect (if, indeed, you had any expectations about our similarities). While not a grammar nerd, I've always felt that improper punctuation leads to the worst of all writing sins: lack of clarity.

Is it possible to use punctuation to do nifty, funny things? Yes, but not easily.

Can it be twisted and used in clever ways to great artistic effect? Yes, but probably not by you. Sorry for being harsh, but it's true—at least until you become a tenth-level master of the dot, dash, and those various squiggly lines.

Which brings me to the comma splice. For example:

> *There was nothing I could do, the path was blocked by*
> *bears with pitchforks.*

Comma splice! (Also, what are the bears doing with pitch-forks? I dunno.)

The reason splices are offensive to many editors is because there's a simple solution: use a period instead. It's basic. Editors, agents, and publishers (not to mention certain readers, wink-wink-nudge-nudge) like to see basics being followed. So instead:

> *There was nothing I could do. The path was blocked by*
> *bears with pitchforks.*

Now, there are other ways to resolve the comma splice. For example, the oft-derided semi-colon:

> *There was nothing I could do; the path was blocked by*
> *bears with pitchforks.*

The reason I feel* the semi-colon works here, is because while the two sentences are each complete, they're also inexo-rably linked. The reason 'there was nothing to do' is *because* the 'path was blocked.' One builds entirely on the other.

You could also rephrase by using a linking word:

> *There was nothing I could do since the path was blocked*
> *by bears with pitchforks.*

As with most punctuation offenses, the solutions can be quick and effective. The trick is taking ownership of your woes and learning to do it right. There seems to be a strange, "I'm just no good at grammar/punctuation/spelling," mentality that happens to some authors. Whether it was being called out at school and embarrassed, feeling like it's 'beyond' them to learn, or plain old laziness, it's upsetting to hear from someone who wants to tell stories that they can't be bothered with the basics. Don't give up, it can be learned.

And …

> *Guess what? If you don't use proper punctuation, your ability to create clear meaning—which is the backbone of effective story telling—disappears in a frustrating jumble of words.*

Phew. Just had to get that off my conscience.

---

* email your semi-colon hate-mail to: aliya@aliyasmyth.com

- D -

DRAFTS

—

Where does one draft start and the next begin?

This has been a huge challenge for me. I like to be organized. I like to know where I am. But I might be on the twentieth 'draft' of Chapter 1 and the second 'draft' of Chapter 18 in the same document. Confuses the heck out of me.

Writing is a process, and each writer will approach it in a slightly different way. It's important to develop a system that works for you, because otherwise it won't work at all. I know this from trying different methods that others use, and while I'm not able to follow their plans exactly, I've learned a lot of great tips on how to stay organized.

One of the biggest lessons for me was to stop back-filling changes while doing a first draft. I now create a plot outline for myself in order to know where the story is going and, more importantly, why it's going there. But a lot of the details in my scenes—character traits, sayings, and the ways the characters interact with each other—comes from inspiration of the moment. In my first book, if I made a change in a later chapter, I would run back and try to change all previous affected scenes.

This is a mistake, because then I got wrapped up in the specific tiny details of the earlier scene. Started beating myself up for all the ways the words didn't work yet. And I used that to distract myself from continuing at a decent pace and getting the damn draft out.

Now I'm committed to seeing a draft through. The simple, yet oh so agonizing challenge, is to keep copious and organized 'fix notes.' As I make a late change, or have a new idea to incorporate, I note where I need to add that alteration in the earlier part(s) of the draft.

If you use Word, you can do this by adding a *comment* (under the Review tab). One nice feature of this is that you can hide them when you want a clean writing space, and they'll disappear from the right side of your screen. Then you can imagine that everything is dandy … until you show them again.

In Scrivener, you can make notes everywhere. Notecards, project notes, document notes for each specific chapter. As I'm starting next drafts (and plotting more stories) it's handy to be able to search my notes. Like any tool, how much you get out of it depends on how consistently you use it, so I'm also trying to be sure to keep the same types of notes in the same places (for example, all plot fixes go on the main chapter notecards).

The other technique I'm using is separating how I name and identify my drafts:

First draft is like mixing the batter. Raw. Just trying to get all the ingredients together. This means it's not for everyone else to eat, but I can take guilty pleasure in licking the spoon and knowing it will be delicious after it's cooked.

Second draft is baking that sucker. Adding heat (that would be critiquers) to turn it into something other people might like to sample. Here is where I try to catch plot holes and streamline clutter—like reducing two minor characters into one. This scary second draft might involve whipping up a whole new bowl of batter, because the original collapsed under the weight of some unseen fault. But it will rise again!

Third draft is about nailing the story. Streamlining action and improving clarity, layering in metaphor (you know, for that deep, chocolatey taste), and plugging any new or overseen plot holes that cropped up since the second draft.

Last, when it's out of the oven, it's time to ice that baby. Um, I don't think I realized I'd baked a cake until just now. It could have been cupcakes, but now it's definitely a big, layered, mouth-watering cake. This is where I do serious line edits. Getting rid of 'that' and 'just' and making the words, punctuation, and grammar pleasing to the palate.

Do I expect everyone to do what I do? Nope. I have my own special brand of strange. I care way too much about the things near and dear to my heart. But find your own process. Make a stew, or a pie, or some wonderful couscous. And please invite me to eat once it's done.

- E -

EMOTION

———

Wow, do I struggle with this.

I don't know how many times plowing through my first draft I heard … *but what's she feeling?* I tried to make sense of that, because, from my perspective, I'd put all the bits in there to show her emotion. Physical signs. Short and angry dialogue. Yet, it wasn't enough.

And I was afraid. Afraid I wouldn't be able to generate any sympathy for my main character.

So I tried to put in 'emotions.' To show the fear or frustration or love my character felt. Like this:

Not enough emotion:
"No, it's not," I snapped.

With lame-ass attempt at emotion:
"No, it's not." My anger could barely be restrained and I bit my lip.

cue rolling of eyes and grinding of teeth

Why emotions are so hard for me to write I'm not sure. Could be the years I've spent developing my cold and rational side and repressing my artistic side. Or it could be that I'm a very visual story-seer. I imagine scenes much like a TV show or movie, where an action carries weight because you can see the expression of the character. However, that doesn't always translate into black and white.

Whatever the reason, action, fight scenes, and dialogue come more naturally than emotions. Plot ideas? I have so many I won't be able to write all the stories I've thought of in the past year alone.

But what good is telling all those stories if my readers can't connect to the characters? To care about their challenges enough to see them from page 1 to page 400?

Despite this struggle of mine, I decided to try and break down exactly what people meant when they said they didn't understand my character's emotional state. And it turns out, what it was wasn't the emotions themselves. It was the thoughts and motivations behind the emotions.

Because emotions are easy to show—it's *why* the character feels emotion that generates sympathy and understanding from the reader.

Once I learned this, the whole thing became a tad less intimidating. I don't need to show the emotion behind every little reaction or line of dialogue. What's important is to draw my reader into sympathy with how the character sees the world—and once they've bought into the character's mindset, they have no trouble fleshing out un-tagged emotion throughout the rest of a scene or book. The key is to figure out the crucial emotional reactions of your character in each scene and fully draw the reader into those moments.

This won't succeed or fail based on one passage. In fact, it's the building of moments between character and reader that strengthens the emotional power of each scene and provides depth as the story progresses.

If you continue to put your character in situations that force them to show their *character*—their goals, struggles, and reasons for reactions—your readers will be pulled further into a relationship with them and will care about the outcome of their story.

I'll bite my tongue there.

- F -

FUCK
AND OTHER SWEARS

———

I'm gonna do it. Here it comes. The words that make your mother cry:

Shoot!
Darn it all!
Well isn't that just a nilly-tickle!

Um. Sorry, that was lame. My character would never say that.

And that's the long and short of my argument in favour of *shit-fuck-cunt-asshole* and whatever other word you like as being the dirtiest of dirties.

If it's in character, use it. Otherwise don't.

You might have a story where such language is forbidden—and that's ok, because then it's not in character for anyone to be using it. They're also probably not skinning dogs, or beheading traitors, or raping villagers.

But if your character is a regular cusser, then to pretend otherwise is going to come across as stilted. Likewise, if you have a character who rarely swears, then when they do it's an immediate identifier of something really, really wrong. That can make for a great character/reader bonding moment.

Now there's some tricky issues when you write historical, fantasy, or science fiction. The cultural context of swearing is so important that using terms which are out of place immediately compromises the integrity of the story. But along with this restriction on the easy-to-access swear, there's great opportunity: making up your own, world-specific curses.

We know that all forms of cussing come from words not meant for polite conversation—which means these can quickly show what is or is not taboo within your society. Body parts and terms for various sex-acts are always popular, as are references to gods and goddesses. Derogatory terms usually come from an observable physical characteristic, often being simple words which time and hate have forged into powerful weapons. An immediate way to alienate two characters is to put them at cultural odds, and vicious smack talk is a quick way to do this. The responses of the characters can also say a lot about who they are and what they consider important.

One thing I've tried to do is to be consistent to both character and world, which I learned from enjoying that masterpiece of gone-too-soon television, *Firefly*. Set in the future, culture has become an amalgam of Western and Chinese influences, with cursing being done in Mandarin. A nice way around the censors. Plus, it also helped cement the flavour of a culture when it might be otherwise difficult to incorporate the Chinese influences without distracting from the story-focused dialogue.

So whatever your world, be true to your characters and setting, and things will be tickety-boo.

Or, fuck it—just do what you want, asshole.

- G -

GENRE

———

When I was a kid, I loved playing with Legos. Still do, come to think of it. Those boxes of unassembled joy promised hours of entertainment … provided nobody put the dragons on the pirate ship or the spacemen in the wolf-army castle. This was NOT ALLOWED!

That hasn't changed because, for me, the world is very discreet, just like each Lego set had its own orderly universe. And that universe mustn't be disturbed.

However …

If there was a compelling reason why dragons would exist in the same world as the pirate ship, I might be inclined to hear you out.

While I value order over chaos, I also value imagination above almost anything else. Using imagination to create and tell stories helps us connect in a deep and meaningful way. I could tell you I like chocolate ice cream, and you might re-member. Or, I could tell you a story about how I once ate an entire tub of chocolate ice cream and made myself vomit brown goo, and you'd think of a story of your own. And now we're having a dialogue.

I'm sure you see where I'm going.

Genre is our lovely, pre-packaged sets of Lego. It's designed to include certain types of pieces, and to be assembled in a way that is familiar and orderly. And it can very much be enjoyed on its own merits, providing hours of creative fun.

But genre is only one way of playing with words, ideas, and story. Sometimes combining genres is the only way of releasing the story you have inside. And that's what has always infected me as a writer—that the story begs to be told not for how marketable it is, but because it has something to say. The characters and themes want to be built regardless of what box they originally came from. My interests range from history to science; pop culture to myth and magic. I think it's natural for the stories I create to be a blend of things that inspire me.

And I'm going to come right out and say it. Sometimes we should stretch beyond the box. The Lego I loved as a child floundered for a while, yet has made a daring comeback—with one crucial change. The marketing is divisive. There was no expectation when I was young that a Lego set would be 'for a girl' or 'for a boy.' The land of Lego had been one of boundless imagination, which wasn't restricted to the body parts you were born with. But now my daughter and son are reluctant to play with certain sets—until someone shows them otherwise.

Likewise, many people become comfortable with the genres they love, and perhaps forget that not every book will adhere to strict genre conventions. Sometimes stories are packaged in the most convenient way possible, with little care for the wider audience they might appeal to, if given the chance.

So that *western* might be a western-fantasy hybrid. And that *romance* may have less kissing and more killing than you're expecting from the cover.

By all means keep the dragons off the space station, but don't forget to keep your eyes peeled for the time when they're the astronauts' last, best hope.

- H -

HOOKS

The word 'hook' is powerful. It immediately conjures an image of that curved, pointed object used for only one purpose: to snare something so it doesn't slip away. Use it for fishing, for lugging meat (you know, creepy meat-locker scene), or to dangle earrings. But if you hook it, you won't lose it.

Who doesn't want to hook their readers? Trap them with words so powerful, they're helpless to do anything except turn the page and read on. All night if necessary.

cue maniacal laugh

But how?

There's no easy answer. If there was, we'd all be spitting out un-put-downable books by the dozen. Certainly, you can't hook all readers with every book. Not even close. But what you can do is try to hook those readers who are predisposed to give you a chance.

Often, when you hook a reader, it's because you've posed a question they want the answer to. This isn't a literal, 'guess what comes next?' question. Rather, it's an emotional reaction to something which has created a sudden, unexpected interest. Because people get bored. Easily jaded. And have short, short attention—

What was I saying?

Oh yeah. So, how do you create this reaction?

One tried-and-true method is to hook readers at the very beginning. Duh, right? But your choice of first scene is critical. Don't tell the readers what you think they need to know. Instead, show them what the world is like through the eyes of someone living in it. Immerse them into a current, immediate situation that forces them to react with a character.

J.K. Rowling did this with the first *Harry Potter*. Even though the first chapter reads much like a prologue, it was filtered through Vernon Dursley, highlighting the strangeness of the magical world by using Dursley's intolerant perspective. We understood both the mystery of the world, and Dursley's character, within moments.

Another technique is to put a unique spin on each character or situation. Make the reader anticipate that interesting things will happen in each scene because of the one before. Write fearlessly. Let your characters and settings find fresh territory. For example, one of my major story locations was a Roman villa and, really, most people are going to congregate in the dining room or garden. However I also branched out whenever I reasonably could. Chicken coops are surprisingly interesting.

This principle applies to characters, too. Let the voice of each one come through, beyond revolving around the main protagonist. Remember that all your secondary characters have lives of their own—goals and interests and fears. Let their perceptions of the world season their motives and dialogue, and they'll add more life to the story.

One last thing to remember: avoid stale bait. Please, please, for the love of all the puppies and kittens in the world, don't open with a dream. You know why that's not a hook? Because you're not being truthful with your reader from the outset. A reader wants to trust that you'll make them gasp with brilliant switches that have been carefully set-up, not because you club them over the head with cliché. Plenty of articles out there list the common faux pas of openings, though just because it's on some reader's (or agent's) *do-not* list, doesn't mean you can't. Just be purposeful in making it shine.

So keep baiting that hook with fresh ideas and hopefully the nibbles will turn into bites.

- I -

INTERTEXTUALITY

—

Well that's a fancy word.

I paid good money to take classes where they talk all about fancy words, but this is one of the few that ever stuck with me past final exams.

Learning about intertextuality was one of those lightbulb moments where I realized there was a word for a concept I'd subconsciously understood, but didn't know how to explain.

So what exactly is it?

Intertextuality is the relationship between two works. That's pretty broad. But it can manifest several ways:

First is when the author purposefully inserts the relationship into the work. Quotes are maybe the most direct method. For example, whenever anyone mentions, "Alas, poor Yorick," from Hamlet, it's an obvious reference to the mortality speech given by the loopy prince. But it goes beyond 'referencing' Hamlet; beyond saying, 'Hey remember this guy?' On a deeper level, it allows a writer to bombard readers with the important messages of other works, just by the merest hint within their own. Other techniques include using similar phrasing as a past work, treating themes in a similar way, or using certain items or settings that the reader will associate with the referenced story.

Second is when the author's subconscious sneaks connections into their writing that they didn't intend. This happened to me, when bits and pieces of other literary works popped out at me after I read my first draft. These weren't characters or scenes—I'm not talking about lifting story here. Instead, they were little references to colours or symbols, or a subtle nod to an event from a work that had a definitive impact on me.

Third is the biggest wild card. This is when intertextuality is created by the reader, instead of the author. A reader will automatically bring their *own* past experiences and knowledge into a new story, and might see a connection which the author had no intention of creating—such a link to a movie the author had never seen. This has a carry-forward effect, which can be good or bad. One that springs to mind for me is that scene in *Family Guy*, where Stewie (baby with the football-shaped head) recites Elton John's *Rocket Man*. Now every time I hear that song, I'll remember that scene, even though *Rocket Man* was written well before the show. They've become linked, the new not forgotten just because you return to the old.

This makes for a six degrees of separation among every artistic work ever produced. In fact, it might even be less than six degrees (probably every work is two degrees or less from Shakespeare—that jerk is everywhere).

But why am I rambling about this? Because how a reader interprets a work is fundamental to how a story is understood. Whether by the intent of the author, or because of the past experiences of the reader, every story will be connected with countless others. Some on purpose, some by coincidence, some centuries and cultures apart.

For the reader, each connection provides them with a deeper, more powerful understanding of the story. And the story will impact each reader in a different way—will become linked with images, works, and thoughts that the writer is powerless to control. Like releasing a balloon into the sky and not knowing its journey or destination. Could end up landing peacefully in the hands of a small child who needed a ray of hope … or end up choking a bird to death on the edges of a polluted lagoon.

Because the reader's mind does not always do what the author intends …

And if you read this whole section as *interSEXuality* instead of *interTEXTuality*, I really must question where your mind is at.

Alas!

- J -

JOB vs. DREAM: FIGHT!

———

I write this section in abject misery, sitting in a coffee shop during lunch break from my soul-sucking job. You know, that thing you do so you don't actually starve while being a starving artist. Yeah, that thing is especially important when you have kids to feed, too.

I was a bit late out of the gate when I finally (re)turned to writing. Like many story-tellers, I loved writing when I was younger. My imagination was so vivid, sparked by my mother's love of all things *Lord of the Rings* and my father's love of all things *Star Trek*. As time passed and pressure to 'pick a career' mounted, I put aside the writerly tinkerings of youth and worked on … well … work.

But story ideas never stopped percolating in my brain until, at last, I realized I just had to do it. Put one word after the other and see what happened. Tell the story that spoke to me.

Then a terrible thing happened.

I loved it.

Oh, sweet words. Story. Conflict. Growth. Climax!

(Sorry, overheated a moment there.)

But my newfound love brought the most dreadful of longings—dreams.

Dreams that I could make a living writing and telling stories. Sharing the ideas I had with others in a meaningful way. Wouldn't that just be the best?!

Reality and dreams are constantly in conflict. To become a writer, you actually have to treat writing as a job. To do that takes time, dedication, and above all, application of craft into actual content. Real books and real stories and real social presence and all the rest of that mumbo-jumbo.

Some people are in the fortunate position of being able to easily balance their dreams with the realities of living. They might have passive income from other sources, or a spouse who makes enough money. They may not have kids, and so have time to get a career off the ground before even contemplating whether that's a path they want to tackle.

On the other side, some people have it even harder than me. Crazy family life that allows for only stolen moments of clickety-clack on the keyboard. Two jobs. Health problems.

Life has its ebbs and flows, and the only thing I've learned trying to balance job and dream is that it's not always possible to do so.

Sometimes, you have to hunker down and scribble a few precious notes on your story during coffee breaks or stopped at red-lights during your commute. Other times, you have to throw off the shackles that bind you to the bank account and immerse yourself in words and dreams. Devote yourself, however briefly, to the intensity of your desires.

During certain, lovely moments, they seem to harmoniously co-exist. Job and dream; work and write. A sweet spot when it all seems possible.

Then the shit hits the proverbial fan (or literal fan, as once happened with goose droppings and the ventilation system at my workplace), and you're back to living under siege and precariously on edge.

But dammit, keep plugging away. Strive to make your word count; your revision deadline; your publication date. One day you might just be able to give up the day-job.

Hey, a girl's gotta dream, right?

- K -

KIDS

—

Writing with kids around is hard.

Writing with *my* kids around is next to impossible. Even simple tasks such as putting on socks becomes a triathlon of bathroom breaks, tantrums, and cannon-fire.

I've heard of miracle babies who play quietly and only cry when seriously injured. I'm not sure such lacklustre angels exist. And I know I'm not alone in experiencing the delights of having high-intensity children.

I'm not being entirely sarcastic when I use the word 'delights.' My kids are amazing. They were early walkers, early talkers, and early-swearers (don't look at me that way). They love stories and produce a volcanic eruption of art every day. Sometimes they just run in circles, providing minutes of enjoyment before someone splits their head open.

More than all of that, I've become a more self-aware person for having them in my life. Their births and growing levels of maturity have made me assess and re-assess myself many times over. The responsibility I feel towards them, and the deeper emotions they've brought out in me have, I think, made me a better writer and—perhaps more importantly—a better human being.

But-oh-my-word-they-don't-shut-up.

When I'm with them, I must forget trying to do anything else meaningful. And that's ok. They deserve my attention. However it makes 'writing at home' a dicey proposition. By the time I've finished my day at work and had some old-fashioned family time, I'm exhausted. Not the best mental or physical state to produce much beyond *Run Spot Run*.

So, how to achieve any balance?

One: I have to commit to the project. This means setting word-count or chapter goals for myself. I work much better with specific goals and deadlines. I've learned over time to be more forgiving with myself when I don't meet them. Because life happens, and right now writing has to fit wherever it can.

Two: I have to get the words out. This means trying to push past the exhaustion on more days than not. It also means not putting crazy pressure on myself to make the words right in the first draft. Rookie mistake was thinking that a book comes out much the same way my papers did in university. Ten pages to be handed in the next morning? Not a problem for the Essay Queen of the North. Stupid idea when writing a book. Fiction readers are much pickier than university professors.

Three: Coffee. Thank you, Starbucks, for free re-fills.

Four: Keep loving it. Keep the passion for each project alive and bright. I write because it's part of me. One day, I hope to share more of that part with my kids. I want to pass on not only my love of story, but the attitude that you shouldn't give up the things you're passionate about. That you can achieve your goals if you put in the effort. I also want them to know that their mom is a whole person herself … not just that voice telling them to get ready for school and to pick up that damned Lego I just stepped on!

(Oh wait, that's mine.)

- L -

LOGLINES

—

Loglines come from the world of film, where time equals money, people! The purpose of a logline is to give a one sentence summary of your story's key elements in order to tempt someone to want more.

If you've ever dabbled in marketing, this is your elevator pitch. The thirty-second attention grabber.

This can be an excruciating task and was HARD for me for a number of reasons. One was that I began writing my first book without a clear sense of the overall plot structure. I had the elements, but I hadn't carefully thought them through. The other reason was that my story was so *amazingly deep* and *complicated*. Yeah I know. Newb. But, in all seriousness, there are deeper themes and elements in my book, and it's more character driven than plot driven. So I struggled for a long time trying to distill the essential character arc—my main character's growth—into something quick and painless to explain.

That's why I've come to see loglines as a great exercise— no matter what type of story you write. You may never feel comfortable using your logline to pitch, but if you work at refining it, a logline focuses your story's crucial elements.

In order to hook your audience, a logline must include tasty bits from four main categories:

1. Your protagonist and who they are. Not their name, mind you, but a quick description of their role and/or status in the world. This gives people a much better connection to the character.

    > For example: *a chocolatier turned government spy* or *a ghost-whispering ex-footballer.*

2. Your protagonist's goal. His goal is, in fact, the essence of the plot. What is the protagonist trying to achieve? This can also take the shape of: what is the protagonist forced into doing?

    > Examples: *searches for his true family* or *must recover her stolen magical lollipop.*

3. The opposition to your protagonist. This can be another character, an organization, or his own inner demons. What is it that is preventing your protagonist from achieving her goal? Because if there isn't opposition, then the story is over in about three paragraphs.

    > Examples: *a terrorist organization* (always a good source of conflict), *a giant gummy bear* (maybe a friend of the Stay Puft Marshmallow Man?), or *his mistrust of others.*

4.   The stakes. What disaster will befall the protagonist, or heck, the whole world? I've seen many writers forget to include stakes, but the threat of specific loss is the most direct way of showing readers why they should care. Without the threat of epic failure, and the sympathy that generates in readers, why bother with the story?

> Examples: *before a democratic government becomes a tyranny* or *before a deadly virus kills her family.*

One last point. Try to make each component of your logline as specific as possible. Sharpen your character, their goal, opposition, and stakes into the clearest focus you can. Then you can write this killer story:

> *A chocolatier turned government spy must recover her stolen magical lollipop to prevent a giant gummy bear's plan to annihilate the citizens of Chocotown with a candy-plague.*

Who wouldn't want to read that?

- M -

METAPHOR
AND OTHER ANALOGIES

———

Metaphor and simile (comparing two, unrelated things with or without using *like* or *as*), are my favourite types of analogy. I use both quite heavily. Even in this book, I've compared writing drafts to baking cakes, and genre categories to Lego sets. And those are the articles I've received some of the best feedback on.

I love seeing connections. It's what helps me better understand the world. When I illustrate a topic using comparisons of seemingly unrelated things, I've seen others make immediate, deeper connections of their own. A new perspective can help someone re-examine what they thought they knew, and apply their imagination to rounding out the analogy. For example:

First drafts are like mixing batter.

That thought leads you to consider how the elements of cooking might be analogous to writing:

Combining ingredients is brainstorming and planning ...
Refining flavor is revising a scene for better effect ...

Within the first breath of linking two ideas, you've assembled the jig-saw of what you knew about each topic and—best case scenario—created new meaning that resonates with you.

I was an avid reader growing up, and voracious consumer of movies and television. I have a wide-variety of interests and experiences (from a hodgepodge of odd-jobs), and have also sponged off others by listening to them talk about their passions. Many of the metaphors I use spring to mind as a natural extension of how I see the world—a bunch of seemingly random things that are in fact intimately connected.

But when writing, the challenge is to use these effectively. To focus my comparisons for certain character view-points. For example, a builder will consider the world from his perspective of understanding construction; a dancer from music and movement. Once you know where a character is coming from, you'll have a better idea of how they would describe the world around them.

The beauty in using analogies is that this technique can be applied to any sort of character. It's not a matter of education or privilege. *Everyone* makes connections. It's a human constant. From the beginning of time, our ability to make connections, and inferences based on those connections, has helped us survive:

Small, red berries poisoned Groog. I should avoid small red berries ... and be really careful with those small white ones that look similar.

So anyone from your humble, not-book-learned blacksmith, to your uppity top tier executive can use metaphor in their dialogue and internal reflections. Careful use by a writer can be a shortcut to drawing the reader into greater sympathy with that character.

Also, use of consistent metaphor can help layer additional meaning into what the character is subconsciously thinking. Two potential love interests can be compared to day and night—to dark and light—without the protagonist even realizing that's the distinction she's making. But it's clear to the reader, and that's what's important.

Metaphor and simile can build powerful descriptions of your world, too.

> *The towers of the castle rose like crooked fingers, gnarled and worn.*

By connecting, instead of outright describing, you can evoke an image that is immediate.

Analogies of all kinds are like constellations in the night sky. They add beauty to the night, meaning among nature's randomness … and guidance when you've lost your GPS. Sprinkle on those sparkles, and let your readers enjoy.

- N -

NEWB KID
ON THE BLOCK

———

It was wonderful being a newb. Everything was shiny and beautiful. My writing was fine—better than fine … *stupendous!* My plotting was spot on and my characters were oh-so-delightful.

sigh

The difference, though, between a newb and a n00b (you know, those hapless morons who can't type and breathe at the same time), is willingness to learn. And at least I had that. I took every scathing critique I got and doubled-down. Read more, re-wrote, and went back for another round.

I can honestly count at least ten revisions of each of my chapters—twice that for the crucial ones. Not to mention chapters scrapped entirely and replaced with something new. Am I a sucker for punishment?

Yes. Yes, I am.

But writing is what I love.

According to Malcolm Gladwell in *Outliers*, I've got to log at least 10,000 hours before I can even consider calling myself accomplished in any endeavour. Author David Eddings said,

"A writer's apprenticeship usually involves writing a million words (which are then discarded) before he's almost ready to begin."

While I disagree that all million need to be discarded, I do agree with the sentiment. To become a master of anything (should mastery of writing even be possible!), you have to put in time, effort, and self-reflection. And if I'm not willing to do that for the work I love—which I hope one day to make my career—then how lasting can my affection be?

We all move through stages when acquiring a new skill. First, it's scary. But we're infatuated with the idea in some way, so we overcome timidity and try. Like a white-belt in a marital art, our first accomplishments seem huge, our first fights legendary! Then you step onto the mat with a blue belt and they black-and-blue-you and send you home to cry into your huge pillow.

Hopefully, somewhere within you or your support system, there's a voice telling you that you can do this. Reminding you that you *want* this, and that taking your lumps is part of the journey.

So you persist.

And every time you bounce back, you discover it's a little bit easier than before. The words come faster and the ideas link better. Yes, you can really see this book coming together at last. Then a black belt spouts off about how there's *quite a difference* between an omniscient narrator and incompetent head-hopping … so you Google gifs of people running head-first into brick walls and find they all look like you.

But, dammit, you persist.

And when you sit back down again, hair standing on end and coffee hooked to your veins, you apply the right words with freakish accuracy, and find ideas which are vivid and enticing.

This is all you can do, and you know what?

It's enough.

As long as you keep at it. Keep trying; keep working. It will be enough.

Am I trying to convince myself? Maybe. But I *am* convinced.

Because the hardest fight I've faced on the way from writing newb to veteran (not that I've arrived yet!) isn't against other writers. It's against myself. Against my sense of failure that I'm not *somewhere else*. I'm not like *someone else*.

That's when I ask myself ... do you love it?

For as long as the answer remains *yes*, then you'd better believe that I'll be all write.

OBLIGATORY SCENES
AND READER EXPECTATIONS

———

Why do we tell a story?

I don't know about you, but I tell a story to share a journey—the one the characters take. Whether that's a literal journey or a metaphorical one, it's a journey nonetheless. And while I'm telling it or reading it, I'm a traveler on that long and winding road, too.

But there's something to keep in mind here. As readers of story, we tend to automatically anticipate a *cause and effect*, because stories, unlike the real world, usually make sense. Instead of situations being random, the struggles of the characters orbit the story's theme the way Earth orbits the sun. While the details of life change year after year, you can be damn sure the forces of the universe will stay constant (science nerds need to stop objecting now—we're working with metaphor here).

There's one force that is the reader's gravity: cause-effect. How does this play out?

First, the cause: a mess of craziness sets the story's conflict in motion. This is the *inciting incident*—the event the protagonist can't turn away from, and which sends her on her journey.

Then, the effect: the conflict raised by the inciting incident is resolved in the climax. Specifically, at least a portion of the climax will be the *obligatory scene*, which reinforces the theme or message the author is trying to get across.

The inciting incident in *The Avengers* is when the baddie steals a portal-making power-source, with the intent to unleash an army of aliens upon humanity. And, since this isn't a Norse tragedy, the obligatory scene is the heroes working as a team to stop said invasion. Theme: When heroes work together, they can defeat any evil.

In *The Breakfast Club* (please tell me you've seen this!), the inciting incident is when high school students from different cliques wind up together in an all-Saturday detention. The obligatory scene is them realizing they have more in common than they thought. Theme: if we look beneath appearances, we can bridge our differences.

Every haunted house movie has an inciting incident where the luckless victims are trapped in the house. The obligatory scene is when they fight their way free, usually by somehow 'releasing' the mean and vengeful spirits. Theme: ghosts are jerks and for-the-love-of-mike don't go upstairs! That's the theme, right?

As readers and watchers of story, we anticipate this structure. And, one way or another, writers need to meet this expectation. This doesn't mean your story has to follow a formula. It doesn't mean you have to rely on cliché. What it means is that you have to be very aware of potential set-ups and their resolutions.

I agonized over this for a long time. Critiquers would say *something* was missing. But what this mysterious thing was, nobody could put a finger on.

This was it:

I wasn't properly balancing causes and effects.

The big resolution? Yeah it was there. But my protagonist's budding romance needed more *cause* for the fallout generated by its failure. And the crucial friendship between her and her foil needed more *effect* in the later part of the story.

Lesson learned. High-intensity incidents need equivalent weight on both sides. If it seems like a crucial set-up to a reader, it needs an effect of matching intensity. Skipping over these things is one of the surest causes of books being flung across rooms in fits of agony ... or of e-readers being smashed.

Let's go back to *The Avengers* for a second. Each of the heroes had a failing. Captain America was a man out of time, hesitant to lead in an unfamiliar world. Iron Man: genius, billionaire, playboy, philanthropist AND 'doesn't play well with others.' Hulk? HULK SMASH EVERYONE!!! To triumph, these heroes need to work together to defeat an evil army. But, when there is no *Iron Man* in *team*, how?

Each hero's failing was called out. Each was forced to confront that failing during the big build-up to the climax. In essence, each hero had a mini *inciting incident-obligatory scene* arc where they were forced to overcome their fault or fail the team. And then they all assemble for the main climax. To me, this is one of the things that made the story so strong. The audience needed those resolutions, otherwise the battle-finale wouldn't have rung true.

But couldn't all of this be seen as (insert dramatic music) pandering?

Some authors resist anything that appears to kowtow to reader expectations. To an extent, I agree. After all, I'm a big proponent of authors being true to their stories. However, authors also need to have the ability to take a step back from their own expectations and look at the story from an outside perspective. To consider what that 'best story' really looks like.

Because if you want to take readers on your journey, you have to pack for their survival. Otherwise, the effect will be readers wandering off the path, never to be seen again.

- P -

PLOTTING
WITHOUT LOSING YOUR PANTS

———

When writing my first book, I didn't really give two figs about proper advance plotting. This character popped into my head, and the main struggles and triumphs she would experience came in glimmers of understanding. I did plot some order of events—mostly dealing with the chronology of her growing up. Working around sporadic writing time for this new 'hobby' of mine meant that I was furiously trying to scribble scenes when inspiration struck (and kids were quiet).

Having now restructured that book, and begun new projects, I've discovered something about my process:

I'm a plan-ster.

Half plotter, half-pantster (you know, the *by-the-seat-of-your-pants* style writer).

Here's why. I need to know where the story is going, partly because I like order, partly because it helps my imagination if I can focus on what I *must* create—rather than having the whole universe spread before me.

However, when I sit down to write, the specific details of scenes come out of I-don't-know-where. Dialogue and character interactions and the little details that make a story tasty. I might be able to plan those one day, but for now, trying to force those out into a plan doesn't work. In fact, it kills my thrill of discovery. My motto:

Plan plot, pants scenes. (Say that ten times fast.)

Why plan plot? Like most aspiring authors, I've done a bit of reading into how stories are structured—and they, by and large, *need* to be structured (see *Obligatory Scenes* if you don't believe me).

That being said, I'm not a fan of the 'formula' approach. As though you can add in a dollop of *save-the-cat* and a dash of *assemble-the-team* and presto! Perfect story. Works for some, not for me. So while formulas might not be my thing, frameworks certainly are, and there's one that works well. Bonus: it's quick to start.

First, understand that what most of us refer to as *plot* is really the journey of the protagonist and supporting characters against an obstacle. So all I have to is decide what they're up against and why this isn't an easy goal to reach. So simple (I wish there was a 'sarcasm font').

While it may not be 'simple,' the first step is clear: decide on the climax. What does the protagonist have to overcome, both externally and internally, for them to reach the conclusion of their journey? That doesn't mean the protag *will* overcome it, just that the ultimate test (or tests) need to be laid out. For example: Luke needs to use both the Force (internal) and his womp rat blasting skills (external) to destroy the Death Star.

After the climax, the next thing I nail down is the inciting incident. This is the first action, failure, or unavoidable disaster that sets the protag on his journey. Staying with Star Wars: Our seemingly average backwater kid, Luke, loses his family to the big bad empire. He must now decide on a path: stay in shit-desert or fight for freedom! How to decide where to start? Try to find an extreme opposite of where your characters are in the climax and work from there. Don't be afraid to make them have true weaknesses, crappy attitudes (like Luke's whininess), and difficult obstacles to overcome (hello, Dark Father!). In fact, make sure those things DO exist.

Of course, this isn't all I do to plan, but it's what gets my creativity rocking. Because after I have those two crucial moments, I can play on the cause-and-effect roller coaster to get my characters through the story.

But then, why pants scenes? If I'm so meticulous, why not try to nail down all the bits and pieces while I'm at it?

Because shit changes.

No matter how great your plot, sometimes that wildcard character enters and smashes the heck out of your best laid plans. And it's fantastic! It hits you in the gut with pure awesomeness and you write until you're barely breathing. You can't take those moments away from me. That's the golden groove when everything under the sun seems to be in perfect harmony. The lightning bolt that ignites the creative fire, and balances the slow burn of endless revising and thankless publicizing.

And then you read it over the next morning and realize it sounds like something pulled out of a fifty-year old fortune cookie.

Whatevs. That's what drafts are for.

- Q -

QUOTES

—

My original thought for *Q* was *Queries*. They are the bane of my existence—my qu-ryptonite, if you will.

(Sorry, couldn't resist.)

When I sat down to distill my experience with queries I realized: I've learned a lot about them; tried countless times (well, maybe actually 40 times), to write one that works; and have over-thought and over-analyzed. But I don't know shit about writing an effective one. I'm learning, but this quest is still in progress.

So, in a quandary, I decided to quit queries in favour of a more positive Q: Quotes.

I love quotes for their compact insight. With one simple phrase, a good quote shines a spotlight of honesty onto our world's stage.

Because everyone has those dark days. You know, when work is shit and family is worse, and someone's eaten that last Rice Krispie square so you ugly cry into your Guinness ... then sob harder because you've watered down your alcoholic escape and now have to stare sober into the black hole of your soul—

coughs

Well, not that that's ever happened to me, specifically.

But when the going gets tough, it helps to know others have been into the dark forest before and lived to tell the tale. Good friends who will help me find the path again. Some of these friends are here today, some I know only through the words they've left behind. But I find solace in the fact that even if I'm one voice among billions, I'm still entitled to that voice.

So here are a few quotes which continue to inspire:

> "It does not matter how slowly you go as long as you do not stop."
>
> ~ *Confucius*

This one always makes me pause and take a deep breath. It has a similar message to that fable about the Tortoise and the Hare, yet reminds me that life isn't a race. It's not about how fast or far you go compared to anyone else. Rather, keep striving towards your own goals in your own time, and you can still get there. Wherever *there* is.

> "Every book is the wreck of a perfect idea."
>
> ~ *Iris Murdoch*

Doesn't seem very uplifting, does it? I'm a perfectionist. It's a blessing and a curse, depending on the day and project. Sometimes I need to remember that artistic endeavors are about taking an insubstantial idea and translating it using imperfect means into the minds of others. That is, in a word, impossible. So quit freaking out about how it's not perfect, dummy. (That's directed at me, though feel free to self-apply.)

"A smooth sea never made a skilled sailor."

~ *English Proverb*

Yep. Life has its storms and waves—tsunamis even. But ultimately, surviving hardships can give us the experience to weather the next with more grit, and the knowledge that we're able to survive, and thrive … and make it to the shore we're looking for.

"I'm just going to write because I cannot help it."

~ *Charlotte Brontë*

This might not be true for every writer, but if I woke up tomorrow with ten million dollars, I would still write. It's part of who I am. The thing my mind does even when I tell it not to. It brings me joy and misery, but I have no intention on being any different.

Which leads to my last quote. (And putting it out there that I'll pay good money—like more than $10—to whoever can *Bill-and-Ted* a dinner party with Oscar Wilde, Mark Twain, and Mae West). From the immortal wit of Mr. Wilde:

"Be yourself, everyone else is already taken."

- R -

REVIEWS

———

I don't understand reviews.

The five-star variety I mean.

My dad used to enjoy watching Siskel and Ebert. That was a review show I could get behind. You got to like the reviewers—saw them as real people with interesting opinions. Over time, you developed a level of trust in their judgments, and eagerly anticipated what they'd say about that big-bang-blockbuster. But I think a huge factor in the success of the show was its simplicity. Thumbs up; thumbs down. Either the movie was worth the time to watch, or it wasn't.

The five star system makes no sense to me because there isn't one scale everyone is following when choosing each number of stars.

Some people give five-stars because they simply enjoyed the heck out of the story. Sure there were spelling and grammar issues by the bucket-load, but the real gold—the story—was fantastic. Other people also love the story, yet will only give the book three stars because the SPAG (Spelling, Punctuation, and Grammar) issues were too distracting. And the real kicker is that not everyone who clicks the little stars will describe why they chose the number they did.

Plus, how biased are these reviewers? Are they all members of the same secret organization (yes, Knights Templar, I'm looking at you)? Friends? It could be that someone's mother is happy enough to open twenty Gmail accounts, twenty Amazon accounts, and buy twenty copies just to write twenty, five-star reviews. Mothers be like that.

Let's not forget the reverse: big bad trolls. Lurking in the shadows. Chuckling as they click the one star button. Their motives are obscure—sometimes they hate the author, sometimes they dislike the genre, and some are that special kind of stoopid where hurting others is all fun and games.

And so we never really know the true story behind all those one-through-five-cluster-constellations.

There's also a difference between 'star votes' and written opinion reviews. I love hearing those! No sarcasm—I truly enjoy being able to read (or listen to) a well thought-out reaction to a story. But, unfortunately, there's one big reason why I don't often read reviews: time. There are so many variables in each reviewer's opinion that I need time to contemplate and weigh them against each other. But I don't have that luxury. So in this world of limited time and unlimited opinion, I often dismiss the lot. Instead, I'll see if the story-concept hooks me; then the first few pages. The book must suit me, after all, no matter how many other people liked or hated it.

Of course, like all authors I selfishly hope that people will leave positive reviews of my books. However it's expected that negative reviews will bloom for reasons from the valid (such as not thinking the book was well crafted), to the inane (it was too long or too short for the price).

All of this brings me back to my point: I don't understand reviews.

I'm deferring to Oscar Wilde on this one: "Books are either well written or badly written. That is all." Sounds to me like a thumbs up/down scenario.

Again, we're dealing with that tricky fellow: *opinion*. But if a book is worth your time, if you become enchanted by the story and captivated by its message, then it must be well (enough) written in your eyes. Only time and an altered perspective may convince you otherwise.

Same for the reverse. If the grammar is so lousy you can't experience that transportive magic which your favourite tomes conjure, then it's poorly written. Stop reading before your eyes bleed. Seriously, put it down. And put the red pen down too. Phew.

Let's keep it simple people. Please? For me? Cause I suck at figuring out what a 2.58-star review means.

SHOW, DON'T TELL

—

Show, don't tell—sounds like an impossibly quiet day in kindergarten.

Along with advice about avoiding adverbs, writers are often given this piece of 'common wisdom.'

The strange thing is, most books I enjoyed reading as a child did far more telling than showing. Some are outright journalistic—like Jane Eyre's, "Reader, I married him." If that's not telling, I don't know what is.

Once again, we're faced with a matter of style and perspective. The one thing that *show* does very, very well, is focus the reader's attention on specific details. The act of describing a feeling, item, setting, or character in greater complexity means the reader senses its importance. *Show* can also immerse the reader into greater empathy with the characters:

Anne walked through the wet grass.

vs.

Within moments, Anne's soft slippers became soaked, the hem of her skirt weighted down by mud as she skidded in the mire of the sopping lawn.

I'm going to balance two important things here.

One: I find the second line more evocative than the first. It gives me a greater sense of what Anne experiences as she makes this trek across the grass. I don't necessarily imagine how her skirt might feel in the first sentence, but in the second I can see how it could become an obstacle ... especially once the werewolf starts chasing her.

Two: In the world of publishing, where everyone seems obsessed with word-counts and bottom line costs, the second example takes about four times as many words.

So the question becomes: is the *show* important?

If the werewolf is about to appear and chase Anne—her impractical slippers failing to gain traction on the slippery grass and her skirts tripping her up—then by all means use *show*. Use it to heighten the suspense and demonstrate how perilous Anne's position is. If word-space allows, *show* can be an effective tool for both immersing the reader and also varying your pace to provide build-up to crucial scenes.

However, if Anne is crossing the wet grass to reach a party, and the party is what's important, then save your *show* for the fancy decorations and drunk guests puking into punchbowls. *Oh! The scandal!*

Every detail doesn't need to be shown, otherwise we'd all end up writing *War and Peace and Comas*.

Picture the balance of show and tell like stage lighting in a theatre. Sometimes you need the whole shebang of flashing light and colour to give each singer, dancer, and set time to shine. But while that might work for the occasional musical number, so much showiness is exhausting when done to excess (disco balls, anyone?). Remember you can also pare back to one spotlight on one character. Focus the brightest beam on the thing that is most important and let the rest fade into the background until it's needed to make a dramatic entry.

If you only use *tell*, readers may *understand* what you've written, but may have difficulty bridging that last gap into the depths of the story. Effectively using *show* lets your readers *experience*, sometimes in intimate detail, the sensation of being a character; of being in a different place and different time.

So keep watch for the scenes you need to expand because the werewolf chase is imminent. And watch out for disco balls because, really, no one wants a Saturday night seizure anymore.

- T -

THEME

———

Theme can be a tough topic, because different authors often have slightly different variations on what *theme* means. Overall, this is how I see it:

Characters are the *who* of your story.

Plot is the *what* and *how*—the events and choices of the characters that lead them from the first obstacle to the last conflict.

Setting is the *where* and *when*.

But theme ... that's the *why*. Why does any of this matter? Why is it important?

Themes are enduring and universal. Revenge vs. forgiveness. Loss of love. Rebellion, duty, and social structure. There are dozens of themes, and even more theme combinations, that a story can address.

Now don't confuse *theme* with *moral.* You know:

> *And the moral of the story is that if you lie, your tongue*
> *will be cut out by angry villagers and you'll be doomed*
> *to an eternity of suffering.*

I outgrew stories with morals when I was eight, and a classmate who lied and cheated on a test won an award for work that wasn't hers. *Fuckit!* My tiny brain learned that day that having morals isn't wrong, however morals only determine what *you* feel about a situation. They don't really affect what others do in the Big Bad World around you.

The older I got, the more I realized that the world isn't black and white—and it's not even fifty shades of gray. *Everyone* has a narrative in their own mind of *good and bad* based on their perspective. While there are some principles most of us humans hold dear, there are also instances where our moral highground dissolves underneath us. A classic case of this is stealing. Stealing is wrong. W-R-O-N-G.

Except for Robin Hood. He's ok, because he was cleverly subverting the corrupt aristocracy—you know stealing from the rich and giving to the poor.

But otherwise, stealing is still wrong.

Weeeeell ... except for Jean Valjean. I mean, he just stole a loaf of bread. And it was to feed his sister's children. Somebody has to think of the children!

So really, stealing is wrong except for all the times it isn't. But by using story to explore the issue of theft, we are encouraged to think more deeply about what we actually believe.

Theme allows you to explore those difficult questions as *questions.* Not as *answers.* Different characters can act in ways that work many sides of a theme. Take *rebellion vs. order*. Some characters can be über-order; others in total rebellion. Many are in the middle, undecided about where their loyalties and values lie. And this is how you explore the theme. Make the reader question their own values and sympathize with characters from all philosophies.

The best stories don't tell the reader *what* to think, instead they encourage the reader *to* think. To question. And ultimately to reaffirm their own beliefs or adopt slightly new ones.

There's one more, crucial importance to theme. Theme is the tool that puts your original stamp on a work. Because we've all heard it: *every story's been written.*

But if you're with me that there are as many perspectives as people, then theme is how you—yes, little old you—can take *seen-before* characters, *seen-before* plot, and *seen-before* setting, yet still write a story that's unique. Because how you approach the story's theme will have never been seen before.

- U -

UNNECESSARY SERIES

Your heart beats faster. Hands shake as you clutch the book, crinkling the pages ever-so-slightly as your rage takes hold.

What's the point?! GET TO THE POINT!

Sigh. But there is no point. Characters are dropping left, right, and center. The fate of the world is on the line. Yet you just don't care. Because you're reading book three of the unnecessary series. You know, that book an author cranked out to meet a deadline and a big promotion campaign, but ended up feeling tacked-on and heartless?

I find many stories, especially those that take place in unique worlds or under a unique premise, pretty much beg for at least a trilogy. The benefit of a series is that it gives both the author and reader so much to explore. Obstacles grow in intensity. Ever-more fascinating personalities get a chance in the spotlight. And, most wonderful of all, when beloved characters die, you cry. (I'm looking at you Dumbledore/Wash/Masterharper Robinton.)

sniff

The flip side is that sometimes authors don't know when to quit. Or at the very least, take a hiatus from the series until the right story presents itself. Yes, that might be harsh of me, and I'll probably have to slap my hand when I find myself pushing for an unnecessary sequel of my own.

I grew up with fantasy and sci-fi series of all kinds—TV, movies, books classic and modern, even comics when I could get away with it (*moms!*). From Star Wars to Harry Potter; dragons on Pern to lords of rings—these are quintessential never-ending stories. The characters and situations are so varied and vivid that you could play in those sandboxes through all the ages of the world and never get bored.

But there's a big difference between an *unlimited world* and *necessary story*. Just because the sand is there, doesn't mean it's the right consistency to make a castle. You need all the other perfect-castle conditions, too.

Which is why, for all the benefits that a subsequent book in a series might have, there are also some serious challenges. It's not just about the stakes rising from *save town* to *save world* to *save galaxy*. In my humble opinion, the success of later books is directly tied to character growth. If the characters aren't growing or changing—being confronted by challenges which force them to stretch and improve—then the story will feel flat, regardless of how many foes they fight or explosions they survive.

Harry Potter had an ideal series dynamic because the challenges increased in intensity in proportion to Harry growing from child to man. He needed to mature to confront these obstacles, and we readers wanted to see how it would happen—how would he succeed? Where would he fail? The literal 'growing up' isn't required, but the tactic of characters taking greater control of their reactions to outside forces, and also taking greater responsibility for others, is an arc that can be built on book after book.

I know you're groaning that I've brought up *Saint Potter*. But it's crucial to remember that Rowling planned her series in advance. Not every step of every book, but she had a very good idea of what the final conflict in Book 7 would entail. Another famous 'trilogy,' *Lord of the Rings*, was never intended to be a series, but rather one book.

So here's my two cents on developing a series:

1. Each book should have its own internal conflict that is resolved by the end, while having elements of a larger plot arc that can remain unresolved until the series finale.

2. The best series are those where the author had at least a vague idea (and often a strong idea) of what the LAST book would look like. The weakest are the ones where the author only had a vision for the FIRST story.

If you're writing a story you think has the potential to become a series, pause. Take the time to plot out what the series arc would look like, which is really just a glorified story-arc.

Like any battle-plan, it may get chopped and revised, or improvised in the heat of the moment. I'll drop an Eisenhower quote here: "In preparing for battle I have always found that plans are useless, but planning is indispensable." That's how you have to approach your series for maximum impact. Plan first, improvise later. Then you can be adding towers to solid sandcastle foundations, rather than trying to shore up a sloppy, too-wet structure.

But if worse comes to worse and you're pantsing your way to a conclusion, don't despair. You may get lucky and have your unnecessary series turned into blockbuster cinema—which will, of course, unnecessarily split the last book into two parts.

- V -

VOICE

—

Finding your voice can be a powerful experience.

As a kid, I was painfully shy. It took me a long time to realize that most people weren't going to bite my head off for voicing a contradictory opinion. And those who did would probably react the same way to any challenge to their authority or world-view. So I've learned to express myself politely (I am Canadian, after all), but also honestly.

Writing was a huge part of that experience for me. By giving my characters voices of their own, and forcing them to speak about their own trials and errors, I developed a deeper perspective on seeing the world through multiple pairs of eyes.

But once I got through about the third revision of my book, an awful thing happened.

I re-read it cover to cover. And, I kid you not, it almost made me physically sick. I felt the whole thing was juvenile beyond redemption.

Craptastic.

Trash-worthy.

Bonfire fuel.

For weeks I couldn't even look at it, convinced it would be a crime to ever subject anyone else to such drivel.

Thanks to some good advice at the right time, I avoided deleting it forever. Instead, I put it aside and probably did the best thing possible. I worked on other stories. A few shorts. Chapters of next novels. I did some plotting and some poetry. Even some nonsense free-writing (that was murder for the analytical side of my brain).

As I started working on another project which had already gripped me, it dawned that my voice had already changed. Not only that, but this other voice would have been unsuitable to my first novel.

By stretching my mental muscle and attempting a wider variety of writing, I learned some wonderful lessons, particularly from short story authors—who are much better at balance than us crazies who tackle novels first. The breakthrough was realizing my style and voice didn't have to be defined by one story.

Authors have voices. However, their voice often makes itself known by *what* the author chooses to write, not necessarily how they write it. The theme and story show the focus of their thoughts and the ways in which they see the world.

Stories have voices. Style of writing, sentence construction, and word choice can and do contribute to these voices, which can vary as the author tackles new projects and experiments with different methods. One book in first person, one in third. One story with long, flowing sentences to match a lyrical narrator. Another with short, direct dialogue.

Characters have voices. These should be distinct, both from the voice of the author, and from the voices of other characters. But character voice must match the tone of the story. No valley girls in Victorian London, if you please.

So now, I'm not so focused on *one* story that I forget there will be other opportunities. Just like Picasso painted in an ever-expanding variety of styles—using different theory, colour, and shape to inspire him—writers can take comfort in the fact that finding their voice is a journey, not a destination.

- W -

WORDS

———

A favourite Mark Twain maxim is:

> "The difference between the right word and the almost right word is the difference between lightning and a lightning bug."

I love words. They can be precise or vague. Used to hurt or heal. And while (sadly) I only write in English, I'm constantly amazed at how diverse and flexible this mixed-ancestry language can be. Even though most of my ancestors never spoke it, I have a particular affinity for English—perhaps because it's as blended as my own heritage. With almost 200,000 words in use, many gleefully stolen or corrupted from other languages, we can play with near-infinite combinations. Yet most of us only use a few hundred words every day.

On the extremes, *Green Eggs and Ham* by Dr. Seuss contains a mere 50 different words, while Shakespeare used more than 31,000 in his collected works.

shakes head in amazement

There are two ways to approach this word-ly whimsy.

The first is to recognize when you're writing for clarity—such as trying to illustrate powerful visual images. This is when it's best to use the fewest number of words that convey the most specific meaning. An endless hunt, because translating something from your brain into a language with many, many synonyms can be a ~~fucking nightmare~~ rigorous challenge.

My personal pet peeve in this regard are words which have multiple, dissimilar meanings. For example:

> Wind: *the perceptible movement of the air.*
> Wind: *move in or take a twisting or spiral course.*
> Wind: *make (a clock or other device) operate by turning a key or handle.*

How the word is used should make the correct definition obvious; however this damn word gets me every time. It's like I have to re-learn how to think after reading it. I dunno why. Whereas other words—such as bludgeon, smile, applesauce—provide very clear mental images.

This leads to the second way of playing with words: being deliberately ambiguous. I'm a fan of characters saying one thing, but conveying something else entirely. Bonus points if it means something different to the reader than to multiple other characters. This kind of dialogue is a natural reaction, not only in social situations—where the pressure to conform only allows for subtle hints of true feelings—but also in emotionally intense scenes where it's much too risky to blurt out, "I LOVE YOU WITH THE PASSION OF A THOUSAND SUNS!" *Awkward.* In these cases, having multiple meanings allows for word-magic. *Abracadabra!*

But, like all good magic, the blood, sweat, and tears happens behind the scenes.

That's what revision is for: adding a flick of precision and a flourish of poetry in just the right places. And giving yourself permission to agonize for hours and hours about two words out of 100,000. I take heart from the fact that because I don't have to show my work to the world until ready, words are a very forgiving medium to work in … even if readers are not always the most forgiving of audiences.

It's also interesting to note that both the works of Dr. Seuss and Shakespeare have become classics, which perfectly demonstrates how there's more than one right way to hat a cat.

> *Alas, poor Yorick*
> *Was a knave*
> *And now I find him*
> *In his grave*

Er. Never mind.

But playing with words involves knowing what you want to say, how you want to say it, and who you are speaking to. (Or *to whom you are speaking*—jeez, take it easy.) Whether that be in language simple or complex, you can find a powerful way to drive home your message.

A last little observation. While I'm a huge advocate for proofreading and editing, it's also the case that an error is bound to slip through here or there. Just do your best and remember:

1. Nobody's perfect; and
2. A typo within a word is less forgiving than the incorrect use of a buzzard.

- X -

XENOPHOBIA
AND OTHER QUIRKS

—

Xenophobia
> *noun* - an intense or irrational dislike of people from
> other countries.

Picture this:

David hates people from Ireland. Hates them. Uses every ethnic slur in the book and a few he learned at his mother's breast. So when Patrick McGowan shows up as his new boss, we know there's gonna be some kind of serious conflict.

Quirks can be useful for a huge number of reasons. As in the example above, they can be a shortcut to ramping up tension by tipping readers off to potential brawls. You can make your characters stand out from each other by anointing them with different physical or behavioural traits—the old everyone gets a peg-leg or an eye-patch trick. Or use dialect or other dialogue ticks to add personality. I mean, who can forget Hodor from *A Game of Thrones*? What a fantastic way to have the reader sympathize with a character whose primary reason to exist is to carry around another, more important, character.

When you start brainstorming unique traits for your various major-agonists and minor one-offs, keep watch for how you can use them to develop scene and character interaction. For example, if we know David is supposed to be at odds with his boss, by having his xenophobic quirk be directed specifically at Mr. McGowan's ancestry, all sorts of potential scenes present themselves. From basic name calling and the trope-ish drinking contest, all the way to Patrick and David being stuck together at the Dublin headquarters of their company during a 'corporate restructuring.' Anything to test David's limits will do, so long as it fits the tone of the story.

But then, imagine that for all David's Irish-raging earlier in the book, no conflict ever brews between him and Mr. McGowan. Well, that's going to be a major bummer for your readers.

Imagine if Indiana Jones never had to deal with a single snake. Or Harry Potter's scar bore no magical meaning—just mentioned often. Or Scarlett O'Hara saying, "Tomorrow is another day," right after eating pancakes. Well fiddle-dee-dee, that would be pretty pointless.

Quirks can be a wonderful way of heightening your story's reality. Because, on some level, we actually do ascribe superficial traits to the people we meet—a shorthand for getting to know them. Like that girl in the office who always tells stories about herself, but never listens to others. Or that guy who always taps his feet when there's music playing, no matter if it's smooth jazz or techno. We notice! And as writers we *should* notice these things. Not because people are only defined by their quirks, but because we have a limited amount of time to describe the uniqueness of any character.

However, don't go overboard and give every character a peg-leg and an eye-patch and a parrot and a shimmering golden hat that whistles in the rain ... that's just quirk-soup. Worse than Animal Crackers and twice as batty.

Keep in mind that quirks are best used to do at least one of two things:

1. Inform the reader about one of the most important facets of a character. For example, a quirk can also be a metaphor for personality. The way Merida's wild, curly red hair in *Brave* was symbolic of her expectation-defying personality; or

2. Impact the story by adding to plot or character development. Like the way Marty McFly's anger at being called chicken (or yellow) makes his situation worse every time he takes the bait and gets suckered into a confrontation. It adds to the drama by vastly complicating his journey back to the future.

Play with quirks and give your characters their own personality. Not only that, leverage those traits into the puzzle of your story. People tend to make friends with those who have some similarities, but who also complete each other's 'missing' portions. One is daring, the other reserved. Like puzzle pieces, together they form a more distinct whole. But enemies ... well those are two pieces that will never fit. Maybe they're shaped alike, or maybe they come from different boxes.

So craft your quirk puzzle with care. Let your characters limp and squint and *ya'll*. Just keep it grounded in what you need to highlight their individuality, without blinding your readers to the story.

- Y -

YOU'LL NEVER WRITE ALONE

——

Yes, I've cribbed this from the club song of Liverpool FC, my favorite football team (no, not that football, the other football—fine, call it soccer). *You'll Never Walk Alone* is the finest anthem a club could have. Don't argue. It's simple and sweet and easy to sing at the top of your voice.

As a writer, you'll meet those who'll play with you, and others who'll play against you. That's life. These opponents may be friends or family who don't understand why this *writing thing* is so important. Some who knew you before you began writing with purpose may never see you as 'a writer' at all.

However the worst opponents are often other writers. They'll likely have a different philosophy of writing from yours. Classic antagonists are artists vs. pragmatics. An artist will often say he writes because the voices in his head compel him; a pragmatic defers to the cold reality of meeting audience expectation and filling her bank-account. Neither of these is a better reason than the other to write, yet they'll argue until blue in the face. Not only that, they will often actively discourage the other.

Writing isn't one game of soccer—where a certain number must lose for others to win. It's not even that pick-up game, you know where one party-pooper grabs her ball and runs home because she doesn't like the score.

Writing is a process, and a passion, and a method of communication.

True, not everyone can become a blistering success. But successes can come in ways big and small to all authors who persist and grow. You start a nobody (well, unless you're somebody's baby, and even that comes with drawbacks). For a long time it feels like all you do is work for scraps—meagre morsels of praise that others can seem so unwilling to give. Because the hard reality of life is that most people aren't going to care about you and your struggles; about the story that grips your soul and the scenes that keep you up at night long past the hour decent people have had their rum and gone to bed.

And why should they care? After all, you're just a minor character—even a nameless extra—in their adventures. But the flip side is, like all great stories, yours will intersect with others who will connect with you. Who appreciate what you can offer and want to offer help in return.

Being open to finding these people was a gigantic challenge for me. I'm a reasonably intelligent human being who strives to be reasonably competent at the things I take on. However, I also use those traits to construct a wall of protection. A way to avoid being taunted or torn down. But you can't live or write—or play soccer—hiding behind a wall. Life isn't a one-person game. So while I might be an introvert at heart, I started letting down my walls, bits at a time, around people who were willing to see past them. And something I never expected happened. I met people who helped me stick out this writer life. In fact, I've made some of the greatest friends of my life. However, I had to be willing to take that first step on the field. To offer help and make connections, one play at a time.

Those people you click with become your allies, your cheerleaders, and best of all, your team members. Pick you up off the turf when you've been tackled hard. Even pass you the ball so you can score. And when you do, they'll be happy for you, not bitterly trolling your Amazon account and leaving one-star reviews. Those are the people you write for, and the people you craft stories with.

So when your dreams are tossed and blown, and you've been downed on the muddy grass, don't be afraid to reach out to the teammates who'll keep your hopes alive. Just as you would willingly run to their aid, so they will run to yours. And you'll never write alone.

- Z -

ZOMBIES
AND OTHER MONSTERS

———

I might get some ire for this but …

peers over shoulder in trepidation

I don't really like 'monster stories.'

Most are written for 'the scare,' but because I don't believe in things that go bump in the night, I have a hard time immersing myself enough to enjoy the fright. (Yeah, I ain't afraid of no ghosts.)

But I love stories about what makes humans monstrous.

After all, that's what's at the heart of most enduring monster stories. *Frankenstein* isn't about how Dr. Frankenstein's big bad creation is super scary. It's about how ethically tenuous Dr. Frankenstein is for making him in the first place.

Dracula isn't about how chill-inducing vampires are—it's about the terror of being seduced by the darkness that resides in us all. About how frightening and damaging it would be to live in a world of unrestrained desire.

That's where I think a lot of people go wrong with their monsters. The scare isn't the creature itself, but rather what the creature represents as a threat to your happiness, sense of self, and sanity.

A zombie could stand there all day, dripping blood and leaking intestinal fluids on your rug. But if you hate that rug (I mean, it didn't pull the room together or anything), then so what?

No threat. Just undead decoration.

Zombies aren't scary because of what they are. They aren't even scary because of what they do—feasting on that yummy gray matter. (I mean, c'mon, lions will eat people too). They're scary because they turn you into a mindless creature, unable to control your own actions or achieve any of your dreams. Zombies represent the ultimate in horrible bosses or—more seriously—the inevitable nature of social conformity.

The threat posed by the monster in question must be all consuming (zombie pun intended). It can't just be after your life, it has to be after your heart and your mind—everything that makes you human must be on the line. And not only that, the threat must be imminent. As in, the characters should really be about to lose right until the very end.

This is why monsters are such an awesome tool for exploring theme and layering on the metaphor. Each monster can embody the extreme of the concept being explored. Frankenstein's monster comes into being as a giant baby—ignorant of the world and his place within it. And this is why Victor is doomed: he doesn't nurture his creation the way a parent would a child, because instead of trying to create life, he's actually trying to cheat death. That is the exploration of theme. Not that making the monster is inherently bad, any more than birthing a child is necessarily good. It's the responsibility and mindset of the person taking on that generative force that affects the outcome. And damn, Dr. Frankenstein really breaks bad after he flips that switch. *It's alive! Wait … you mean I actually have to take care of it? I'm outta here.*

That's the struggle we face when confronted by our most frightening opponents. They seem overwhelming—evil-dead-hoard overwhelming. The dark is deep and the light is but a flicker in the distance. Our tools are not enough. Our plans and happy-ever-after dreams are not enough. Not on their own.

So when you decide to sculpt your nightmares at last, and breathe words of life into their actions, don't forget that it's easy to make them *many*, and even easier to make them *powerful* … but the key is to make them attack the very thing your characters hold most dear. Whether that's the foundations of the society they live in, or the bodies of the family they love, cut right to the heart of your protagonist's deepest fears.

You could probably go a long way with a monster that sucks every last cent out of your characters' bank accounts, and turns them into indentured slaves for the rest of their lives.

Oh wait, those are called children.

ALPHABET ARCHIVES

One tremendous thing that's happened since writing this book has been other authors sharing their own stories and struggles. When you write, you sometimes don't know if what you're saying will have an impact on anyone else. So for the feedback on this little labour of love to be both positive and personal, is truly inspiring.

If any part of this book resonates, I'd love to hear from you. That's why I've created the Alphabet Archives on my website:

www.aliyasmyth.com/alphabetarchives

It's my hope that the stories and comments collected there will be an inspiration for all us authors in agony while we work towards our goals.

And you can always drop me a private line at:

aliya@aliyasmyth.com

RESOURCES

You can't write in a vacuum. Well, you could, but it would be windy and dusty. When you think your writing sucks, sometimes you need a few ideas to get flowing again. A few choice pickings of mine:

FOR WRITING

You Can Write a Novel by James V. Smith, Jr., for down-to-earth help with the nitty gritty of getting a story written.

The Anatomy of Story: 22 Steps to Becoming a Master Storyteller by John Truby, for a classic take on story structure that lets you tackle plot from either character or premise.

Wired for Story by Lisa Cron, for showing that we do, in fact, actually experience story as though we are living it ourselves.

The Storytelling Animal by Jonathan Gottschall, for illuminating how story is an essential part of our humanness.

Dan Wells on Story Structure, YouTube Videos, for a simple to follow structure that's flexible for many kinds of plots: https://youtu.be/KcmiqQ9NpPE.

FOR THINKING

Outliers by Malcolm Gladwell, for linking small ideas with big impacts, and other general coolness.

Sex with Kings by Eleanor Herman, for getting people into the bedrooms of history and uncovering a new perspective on sexual politics.

Guns, Germs, and Steel by Jared Diamond, for tying together the dangling strands of history.

FOR STORY

The Song of Achilles by Madeline Miller, for beautiful, precise sentence structure.

The Seventh Son by Orson Scott Card, for imaginative and immersive descriptions of a real-world magic.

The Lord of the Rings by J.R.R. Tolkien, for being the granddaddy extravaganza of world-building.

Frankenstein by Mary Shelley, for being the original science fiction, and a damn fine read to this day.

Rome, the HBO mini-series, for giving as much screen time to the nobodies of history as to the immortal names.

The Harry Potter series by J.K. Rowling, for an amazing demonstration of how secondary characters give story life, purpose, and heart. Always.

And last, but not least:

The Monster at the End of this Book by Jon Stone, for being the first book I memorized cover to cover, with an ending that makes me laugh every single time.

ACKNOWLEDGMENTS

I want to give a brief, yet extremely heartfelt shout-out to Calliope, my muse, and in particular to her minions Alexander Qi, Rebecca Carter, and Erin Merrill. Without your support I might have dropped the writer's mantle, as it can be a heavy burden for those who take it too seriously.

To Emme Wright, for her unfailing support and astute questions as I chopped my way through the early drafts of these letters. You push me to be better, while also ensuring I always feel as though I'm good enough. A rare friend indeed.

To my hubby, Kevin, for being a writing widower, and taking such beautiful care of our kids and my diet. I might not eat if it wasn't for you.

And to my lovely offspring, whose keen imaginations and audacious personalities keep me on my toes … and loving every minute of it. Well, except for that one time—you know the one. We'll never speak of it again.

ABOUT THE AUTHOR

Aliya Smyth lives on the Canadian prairies, a land so flat you can see your dog run away for six days. When she's not daydreaming about visiting countries with visible topography, she writes speculative historical fiction and fantasy. She is a huge fan of all things fairy tale, topsy-turvy history, gritty literary, and anything that fires up her imagination.

Her first novel, set in Imperial Rome, could be described as a vampire story ... in the same way you'd consider Frankenstein a zombie tale. No magic, but plenty of mayhem abounds for one girl growing up Roman, and surrounded by *Blood and Circuses*. Scheduled for release in 2016.

Read more about forthcoming books, and other strange musings, at aliyasmyth.com.

www.ingramcontent.com/pod-product-compliance
Lightning Source LLC
Chambersburg PA
CBHW021134020426
42331CB00005B/773